The tithe

Elmer Bryan Stewart

Alpha Editions

This edition published in 2023

ISBN : 9789362094605

Design and Setting By
Alpha Editions
www.alphaedis.com
Email - info@alphaedis.com

Contents

PREFACE.

There has been no attempt in this brief work to record every mention of the tithe that may be found in ancient writings. Some have called attention to a large group of references which lie in the era contemporaneous with the history of Israel. Items of history, for example, from 500 to 800 B. C. are interesting, but would not add materially to the argument. In a way they may help to solve the question as to the meaning of terms used in the pre-Mosaic period. Many prefer to be cautious about asserting that there was a religious tithe in this remote period. Mr. Johns in his valuable work, "Assyrian Deeds and Documents" Vol. III, says, for example, (pp. 347-349), that to translate a certain word "tithe" as some do is to "assume that there was a tithe." He admits, however, that this view "agrees admirably with that universally adopted custom among Semitic peoples of paying a tithe to the government." On the other hand Prof. Sayce positively asserts that there is a word which should be translated tithe. The cautious ones say that he jumps at conclusions. Some who do not jump stand ever still and reach no conclusions. Which is better, I do not undertake to say. It has been the aim of this work to take a broad view of tribute, not distinctly as paid to a priest, but to kings as well. Rulers often assumed the function of a priest and appropriated the revenue to themselves. While the meaning of terms and the use of revenue may be in a somewhat doubtful state, there seems to be no question but that the proportion of the tenth prevailed as has been stated.

Acknowledgment is gratefully made of the kind help of Dr. R. F. Harper, Prof. of Assyriology, and Dr. J. H. Breasted, Professor of Egyptology in the University of Chicago, for valuable direction as to books that might be read to advantage. I desire to express my appreciation of the advice and encouragement of Mr. Thos. Kane and other friends who have urged me to present this study to the public. I trust it may increase the tribute to the King of glory, the Head of the Church.

E. B. STEWART.

Chicago, August, 1903.

INTRODUCTION.
WHAT WE OWE, AND WHY WE DON'T PAY IT.

No one not an unreasoning optimist believes that with our present methods of Church finance, it is possible that the World will be Christianized during the Twentieth Century. No one not an unreasoning pessimist believes that if all Christians practiced the Tithe System and devoted one-tenth of their income to the Master's work that the World could not be brought to a knowledge of Christ within the next one hundred years. These two facts being conceded, and no thinking man will deny them, three questions suggest themselves:—

1st. Who is most to blame for present conditions?

2nd. The Results,

3rd. The Remedy.

Answering the first question as to who is most to blame, it is my deliberate conviction based on more than twenty-five years varied experience and growing more decided each year, that the blame very largely lies at the doors of our Theological Seminaries and Theological Professors, the teachers of our teachers. They must bear a very large share of the responsibility.

There will be, there can be no permanent change for the better while our religious teachers are taught to teach us a lot of generalities which do not have even the merit of being glittering on this, of all subjects connected with the Christian life of laymen and lay-women, the most important.

There will be slow progress so long as such a large proportion of students for the ministry are taught that we laymen and lay-women owe everything to God in general but nothing in particular, nothing definite; that the time of payment, manner of payment, and even the amount of payment of whatever we owe, or think we owe, or somebody else tells us we owe, is left entirely to our natural disposition to benevolence or stinginess or to our moods and caprices. That *payment* to God of any definite proportion of our income does not enter into the Christian system; that all our benevolences are to be classed under the general term of "Giving," thus placing our Heavenly Father and the street beggar to whom we may give a few pennies, in the same category. That it is right and not an insult to the Almighty to teach us that we can *give money* to God; that the basis and foundation of the Christian system of providing means for carrying on the Master's work in discipling all Nations is founded on a few sentences from a letter Paul wrote to the Christians in Corinth, urging them to make a generous free-will offering in aid of some suffering fellow Christians down at Jerusalem. For obvious reasons, the reason he gives for urgency in the matter is very rarely quoted: "That there be no collections when I come." Paul evidently had his share of human nature, and special collections which most Ministers so much dread was probably also his pet aversion.

During the past year I have had a very striking confirmation of this opinion. On September 29th, 1902, I sent a copy of the following letter to the President or leading official in each of the Evangelical Theological Seminaries in the United States and Canada, 152 in all:—

Dear Sir—By this mail I send you a sample package of such literature as I publish on the subject of "Honoring God with our Substance." I will take pleasure in sending gratis, express prepaid, a sufficient number of similar packages to supply one for each theological student under your care if you or some one in your institution will state how many will be required and agree that they shall be placed in the hands of the students. Hoping to hear from you, I am

Yours very truly,

Just twenty-seven accepted the offer, thus showing that nearly five-sixths of those to whom the letters were addressed were not willing or indifferent as to whether the students under their care should be taught that the debt we owe to God means anything definite.

In November of the same year I sent a similar letter addressed to the "Professor of Practical Theology" in the 125 institutions where the first offer was not accepted. A total of 22 responded and expressed a willingness some of them an earnest desire to distribute literature on Tithing among the students. Next I tried to reach the students direct, as I had failed to reach them by the first two methods in more than two-thirds of the Seminaries of our country and Canada. Once more I had written and personally signed 103 letters, the envelope being addressed "To That Student Most Interested in the Subject of 'Honoring God with our Substance.'" The letter enclosed was as follows:—

To the student receiving this letter:—

Dear Sir—By this mail I send you samples of such literature as I publish on the subject of "Honoring God with our Substance." I will take pleasure in sending gratis, express prepaid, a sufficient number of similar packages to supply one for each Theological student in your Seminary, if you will state how many will be required and agree that they shall be placed in the hands of the students.

When you engage in your life work you will find no subject of such vital interest to laymen, and a thorough understanding of it, and ability to explain it, will greatly aid you in Church and Missionary support.

Awaiting your reply, and hoping for your co-operation, I remain

Yours very truly,

To my great surprise only ten accepted this offer, leaving 93 institutions devoted to training preachers either indifferent or unwilling to permit their students to accept and read, without expense, the same literature on the subject of Tithing that active Pastors have ordered in quantities aggregating many millions during the last 27 years for circulation among their people.

In contrast with so much apathy and indifference or opposition, many of the replies received were of the most encouraging character, the writers expressing deep interest in the subject and promising hearty co-operation.

Another obstacle, and second only in importance, is found in the attitude of a large proportion of the editors of our Religious Newspapers. It should be remembered in their behalf that nearly all of them are Ministers, and as a result are themselves the victims of false teaching or no teaching on this subject, which to at least nine-tenths of their constituency, is of the most vital importance. The few lay-editors of Religious Newspapers that I have the honor of knowing all believe in and practice the Tithe System.

As in the case of Theological Teachers, I have very recent confirmation of this opinion.

A year or two ago a fellow worker in this field, the Rev. Henry Lansdell, D. D. of Morton College, Black Heath, England, an extensive traveler in Oriental countries, and noted author realizing that Religious books are read by so few people as compared with Religious newspapers, conceived and put into execution the unique idea of publishing serially in slip form suitable for printers' proof, some of the results of the latest archaeological researches and discoveries bearing on the subject of Tithing, supplementing and enriching them with his own researches and interviews with eminent archaeologists. I copy from a letter received from him dated July 8th, 1903:

My Dear Sir—Your letter of the 23d June, quite cheered me. I have circularized and sent slips to upwards of 1,250 editors in 114 countries, Kingdoms and States, sending also with my offer in 167 cases an autograph or dictated letter. Thus far the result is approximately as follows: No answer received from 976, and the number who have declined is 248, whilst about 26 have accepted the series in whole or in part. The number of copies printed of four of these publications amounts to over 400,000 weekly; of the rest I do not know the circulation, but supposing that each paper has four readers, it does not seem at all an extravagant estimate that the articles will be brought before two million readers weekly. This surely is something to thank God for!

Out of the 1,250, more than half were sent to America and Canada. Not one Canadian paper thus far has accepted, but in the United States the papers accepting are California, 1; Arkansas, 1; Texas, 1; Ohio, 2; New York, 1; New Jersey, 1; Pennsylvania, 1; Illinois, 1.

It is my belief—certainly my hope—that Dr. Lansdell has in preparation a volume in which he will exhaustively treat of the early history of the Tithe.

Unfortunately I have mislaid the first three slips, each about a newspaper column, sent me by Dr. Lansdell, and hence am unable to give their titles. Commencing with the fourth, the titles are as follows:—

   IV. Egyptian War Tithes.

   V. Pre-Historic and Spartan Greece.

   VI. Græco-Persian and Later Greece.

  VII. The Romans.

 VIII. The Pelasgi, Britons and German-Saxons.

   IX. Where Did Abram Learn Tithing?

   X. Jacob's Vow.

   XI. Israel's First Tithe.

  XII. Israel's Second, or Festival Tithe.

Naturally the first three would have reference to the very earliest history, including lately discovered evidences of Tithing in pre-historic times.

One would suppose that such original and late matter as these titles indicate, prepared by a thorough scholar, would be gladly accepted and published by the religious press. That it is not carries its own comment.

My own experience has in some respects been similar. To illustrate: Two or three years ago I offered for a limited time to send gratis, express prepaid, to Christian Endeavor societies, Epworth Leagues, and Baptist Young People's Unions such literature as I publish on the subject of Tithing sufficient to furnish one of each to every family represented. I had the offer printed, occupying about an inch of newspaper space, and sent it with a personal letter asking publication to practically all the Evangelical religious newspapers in the United States and Canada. I kept no accurate record of the replies, but probably one-fourth, possibly one-third, cheerfully published the offer; two or three editorially called attention to it, while a few returned it with an offer to insert it at regular advertising rates. The rest ignored it.

As to Results. These, judged by any fair standard are not only deplorable, but a shame to our profession as Christian men and women. The old lady who boasted that she had been a Christian for twenty-five years and had never failed to give a dollar a year to Foreign Missions was a good deal above the average. If she had given a like sum, less than ten cents a month, to Home Missions, she would not have suffered by comparison with the rest of us; and yet we are the richest nation in the world, and while now passing through a season of unexampled prosperity, our gifts to Missions show very slight increase; in many cases they are less than ordinary. No wonder the world sneers at our profession of love for Christ and desire to see His Kingdom established throughout the world. They have the right to sneer in this regard and we are the last people in the world who have a right to criticise them for doing it.

In this respect both our Heavenly Father and the world about us occupy the same standpoint of judgment. No matter what our profession may be, both God and the world measure our real interest in this as in all other subjects by what we do for it, and for us laymen and lay-women our doing is measured rightly and of necessity by our contributions, the money we give.

So far as we are concerned I can think of but one excuse. I admit that it is a poor one but it is the best we have. We have either been wrongly, or insufficiently, taught by our religious teachers regarding this of all subjects to us the most important. There has been little or no "Thus saith the Lord" about it; nearly all our teaching has been on the line of 'Give, Give, Give'; very little of definite *payment of what we owe* and letting free-will offerings commence after our debt has been paid. We have been continuously and persistently taught that we can *give* money to God. We have even been exhorted and urged to be systematically benevolent in the matter of gifts to God. Think of it! Systematic benevolence applied to our Heavenly Father. The whole system of our teaching on this subject has been based on "Giving," everlastingly "Giving." If this teaching is right we laymen can justly claim the right to *give* what we please and *as* we please. Gifts and payment occupy very different standpoints. If I owe a debt, it is a definite amount and I must pay it when it is due, or be branded as a defaulter, but no man *owes* a gift. True, we both give and pay when we pay Tithes, but the payment is to God, the giving as His stewards and agents is to our fellow men for the upbuilding and advancement of His Kingdom.

It is only fair in this connection to say that ministers have the same excuse, poor as it is, that we laymen and lay-women have. They have been the victims of wrong teaching by their professors of theology and teachers of practical— not theoretical—religion. The only sensible thing for us all to do is to repent and reform.

That I may not be accused of overstating or misrepresenting the situation, I copy the Pledge of the Tenth Legion of the Christian Endeavor Society. This Pledge has been signed by over 25,000 of the young people of our churches. It clearly perpetuates this false teaching and will of course bear its legitimate fruit. At the time the Tenth Legion was started the attention of its officers was called to the mistake as I regard it in the language, but they declined to change it. It reads as follows:

"Unto God the Things that are God's"

Enrollment Blank.

Please enroll my name in

THE TENTH LEGION

of the United Society of Christian Endeavor as a Christian whose practice it is to give God the tithe, and send me the Certificate of Membership.[A]

Another result is that while this is a Giving Age as never before in the history of the world, the Church is not getting her share. Christians are giving largely, but not to Church objects nor through Church channels. There are tens of thousands, probably hundreds of thousands, of Tithe Payers but their Tithes are not brought into the modern storehouse, the Church, but are directed into numberless other channels. Habits of giving to objects of benevolence outside the Church are being formed, especially by the young, which will last for life. The result is and will continue that taking into account the increase in wealth and increase in Giving in other lines, the Church is not only not making advance but relatively retrograding.

A further word about the results of this teaching. The Supreme message of Christ was unselfishness. Judging by what we professing Christians give to spread His Name and Kingdom outside of our own churches, which means Home and Foreign Missions, could anything appear more intensely selfish than modern Christianity in rich America? Boiled down, it certainly appears to mean to the world at least, and I fear to God, get converted, confess Christ before men, join the church, attend church and prayer meetings, do as little as you can and be respectable among your neighbors towards the support of your church and pastor, and then give less than $2.00 each per member to Home and Foreign Missions. Yes—taking out the amounts contributed by, say, 20 per cent of generous givers—mark I do not say large givers, it is less than 50 cents each, or to be liberal less than 5 cents each per month for the conversion of the world at home and abroad, and all this in free, rich America. In most other countries Christians have some excuse for not paying the Tithe to God. In most of them there is a State Church, and the State claims the right to enforce payment of the Tithe for the support of that Church. Not so with us. We have no State Church, and are accountable to

God only for the payment of the Tenth. As Mr. Stewart explains in the following pages, the Tithe is God's law for the race, yet the payment—in American churches at least—is entirely voluntary. In this respect it does not differ from the law of the Sabbath, or any other of God's laws. We may refuse to obey any or all of them. Our obedience is voluntary, but our refusal to obey does not abrogate or repeal the laws.

I was rejoiced when I learned that Mr. Stewart, the author of the following pages had been studying this subject for years. I urged him to prosecute the work, and publish the results of his investigations and conclusions. I had the pleasure of reading the manuscript before publication. I regard his work as excellent from every standpoint, and the best for "plain people" I have ever seen. It will be both my pleasure and duty to give it the widest possible circulation, and I bespeak for it careful and prayerful reading, more especially on the part of my brother laymen who are seeking to know and do their duty in this the most important practical subject connected with our Christian life under Twentieth Century conditions.

As to the remedy. There is no immediate remedy in sight. It is simply a question of more light, but light never enters into purposely darkened rooms.

In so far as Mr. Stewart's little volume comes into willing hands it will help take down the shutters and let the light into hitherto darkened rooms. I hope and believe it will also cause many putters-up-of-shutters to hesitate and at least be neutral rather than continue their thus far darkening work.

When the teachings of this little volume, and others yet to be published in the light of recent investigations and discoveries have had time to permeate and leaven the thinking Christian public he will be not only a brave, but a rash, professor, or teacher or editor who will at once advertise his ignorance and offend a large proportion of his pupils, or readers, by proclaiming the doctrine that the Tithe is not God's law for the human race and as enduring as its author. He will not have the courage to teach that it was a Mosaic institution, that it was abolished by Christ, and that Christ intended to substitute in its place as a system of church finance the earnest plea of one of his followers 30 or 40 years later for a generous free-will offering from the churches in Corinth to relieve the needs of suffering fellow Christians in another city.

A natural question would be—"Do you expect that the character of the teaching of a large majority of the Theological Professors and writing by editors of the religious newspapers, most of them past middle life, will be changed by the change in Christian public opinion on this subject, and that they will become active teachers of the binding obligation of the Tithe?"

I have no such hope, but I do hope and expect that they will be neutral and refrain from opposing. My belief is that active opposition and indifference can and will be stayed; but my hope is in the next generation of professors, teachers and preachers, and as a result a generation of laymen and lay-women who will teach and practice that the Tithe is—not was—God's law for the human race, and that the obligation to pay it is as binding now as it ever was.

LAYMAN,
310 Ashland Boulevard.

Chicago, July 29, 1903.

ITEMS OF HISTORY.

"Tithe" is an Anglo-Saxon word meaning "the tenth." Technically speaking, it is defined as "the tenth of produce, property or spoils dedicated to sacred use." Trench quotes with approval Emerson's characterization of language as "fossil poetry" and adds, "but it may be affirmed of it with exactly the same truth that it is fossil ethics or fossil history. Words quite as often and as effectually embody parts of history, or convictions of the moral sense, as of the imagination or passion of men." While this is true of words in such a fascinating way, it will, no doubt, furnish the best basis of conclusion, to trace the history of this word and the principle which it involves. If a word embodies history, the history of a word may contain much information of value. This word then will briefly be traced in both Biblical and Extra-Biblical History.

FIRST: In Biblical Record it appears early. Its *first* distinct mention is in Gen. 14:20. Abram returning from the slaughter of the four kings was met by Melchizedek, king of Salem, and priest of the most high God. He blessed Abram, who in turn recognized him as his priest before God, and "gave him tithes of all" the spoil.

Its *second* is in Gen. 28:22. Jacob had been to the gate of heaven, and none other than Bethel could be chosen as a name for that place. Here Jacob under the impression of the awe of God's presence, vowed a vow, saying, "If God will be with me, and will keep me in this way that I go, and will give me bread to eat, and raiment to put on, so that I come again to my father's house in peace; then shall the Lord be my God; and this stone which I have set up for a pillar, shall be God's house; and of all that thou shalt give me I will surely give the tenth unto thee."

The *third* use is in connection with the Levitical law. The Lord spake through Moses and gave this commandment, which is most fully stated in the three following places:

First: Lev. 27:30-32: "And all the tithe of the land, whether of the seed of the land or of the fruit of the tree, is the Lord's: it is holy unto the Lord. And if a man will at all redeem ought of his tithes he shall add thereto the fifth part thereof. And concerning the tithe of the herd or of the flock, even of whatsoever passeth under the rod, the tenth shall be holy unto the Lord."

Second: Num. 18:26, 30, 31: "Thus speak unto the Levites and say unto them, When ye take of the children of Israel the tithes which I have given you from them for your inheritance, then ye shall offer up a heave offering of it for the Lord, even a tenth part of the tithe." "Therefore thou shalt say unto them, When ye have heaved the best thereof from it, then ... ye shall eat of it in every place, ye and your households; for it is your reward for your service in the tabernacle of the congregation."

Third: Deut. 14:22, 23, 28, 29: "Thou shalt truly tithe all the increase of the seed that the field bringeth forth year by year. And thou shalt eat before the Lord thy God in the place which he shall choose to place his name there, the tithe of thy corn, of thy wine, and of thine oil, and of the firstlings of thy herd and of thy flocks; that thou mayest learn to fear the Lord thy God always."

"At the end of three years thou shalt bring forth all the tithe of thine increase the same year, and shalt lay it up within thy gates: And the Levite (because he hath no part nor inheritance with thee), and the stranger, and the fatherless, and the widow which are within thy gates, shall come, and shall eat and be satisfied; that the Lord thy God may bless thee in all the work of thine hand which thou doest."

How long the Mosaic order was carried out we do not know. Samuel in his protest against Israel's asking for a king (1st Sam. 8:15,17), tells them that "he will take the tenth of your seed and your vineyards and give to his officers and to his servants." "Also he will take the tenth of your sheep; and ye shall be his servants."

It is likely that the sacred use of the tithe was early perverted under the kings. We hear no more of this system until the time of Hezekiah (726 B. C.), who instituted once more "the courses of the priests and Levites" (2d Chron. 31:2-5, 10-12), and "commanded the people that dwelt in Jerusalem to give the portion of the priests and Levites." The people responded at once, "and the tithes of all things brought they in abundantly." So abundant were they that the chief priest reported that, "since the people began to bring the offerings into the house of the Lord, we have had enough to eat and have left plenty: for the Lord hath blessed his people, and that which is left is this great store." So great was this store that chambers in the house of the Lord were prepared for it, and men were appointed to oversee this surplus, who "brought in the offerings and the tithes and the dedicated things faithfully," and kept them in the places prepared for them. Before this reformation Amos had sounded his warning in these ironical words. Amos 4:4,5: "Come to Bethel and transgress; at Gilgal multiply transgressions; and bring your sacrifices every morning and your tithes after three years: for this liketh you, oh, ye children of Israel, saith the Lord God."

The prophets cry out all along the line against the greed and selfishness of the people. The captivity even did not burn out this root of evil, and Nehemiah is called upon to right the neglect of the command, "Honor the Lord with thy substance." (Prov. 3:9.) He joins with the people in a determination to bring the first-fruits and the tithes unto the priests and

Levites, that (Neh. 10:37, 38, 39) the "Levites might have the tithes in all the cities of our tillage." "And the Levites shall bring up the tithe of the tithes unto the house of our God." "And we will not forsake the house of our God." But fickle Jewry was soon denying the charge of robbery at the mouth of Malachi who says: "Ye have robbed God in tithes and offerings and are cursed with a curse." (Mal. 3:10.) "Bring ye all the tithes into the storehouse," that blessings, spiritual, temporal and national, may be poured out upon you. What Malachi denounced, Nehemiah rectified by one bold stroke. He gathered the Levites and singers from the fields, whither they had gone to earn a livelihood, and set them in their places. Once more the old order was restored, and it was true that all Judah (Neh. 13:12) "brought the tithe of the corn and the new wine and the oil unto the treasuries."

When the New Testament opens its pages of history we find the tithe principle very scrupulously observed by the "rigidly righteous," and perhaps by a majority of the Jewish people. The 7th chapter of Hebrews makes use of the word tithe to show that the priesthood of Christ, who is after the order of Melchizedek, is superior to the priesthood of the Levites, because they in the loins of their father Abraham paid tithes to Melchizedek. Barring this chapter there are just six other places where the tenth, or tithe, occurs. Three of these (John 1:39; Rev. 11:13; 21:23) are simple numerals. Of the remaining three, two refer to the same incident as recorded in Matt. 23:23, and Luke 11:42. The well-known words of Matthew, who gives the fullest statement, are these: "Woe unto you, scribes and Pharisees, hypocrites! for ye tithe mint and anise and cummin, and have left undone the weightier matters of the law, judgment, and mercy, and faith: but these ye ought to have done, and not to have left the other undone." The other reference is equally well-known and occurs in the prayer of the Pharisee, who said, (Luke 18:12.) "I give tithes of all that I get." The Revised Version is used in giving these quotations because it more correctly translates the verb in the first references which should also be translated "tithe" in the last reference, for the Greek verb is the same in all three.

SECOND: The Extra-Biblical records have frequent references to the tithe, the number and extent of which can only be hinted at in the brief selections given.

Since the time of Selden who wrote his famous "Historie of Tithes" almost 300 years ago (the edition to which I have access was published in 1618), little seems to have been added to the historical data respecting the tithe by those who write upon that phase of the subject. Every reference book in the various libraries of this city, and all the literature on the tithe, so far as consulted, have the same stereotyped references, with slight variations in supposition and inference. This fact led to the query, "Is there no new data? Have excavators and translators of other literatures discovered no evidence of this usage"? About four years and a half ago, I set about the task of reading in translation all that was available of the mass of material furnished us through the labors of such men as Dr. Legge, Prof. Max Mueller, Prof. Sayce and many others of the worthy host of oriental scholars. A few of the most interesting are given of the items that came to light in the course of a somewhat extensive and at times tedious reading.

In the literature of ancient China, (Li Ki, Book III., Ch. II., Sec. 27) we find this statement: "A tenth of the year's expenditures was for sacrifices." Simcox (Primitive Civilizations, Vol. II, p. 36) comments as follows: "This is nearly the only recognition of a tithe for religious or quasi-religious purposes in China and probably represents a very ancient fragment of tradition. The king received a tithe of the national produce, and he may have been anciently expected to spend a tithe of the revenue so obtained upon the rites of public worship; but an earlier passage in that same book describes the Son of Heaven as retaining nine-tenths of the produce of his domains for his own use, and employing the other tenth to defray the charges of the public offices."

Prof. Maspero (The Dawn of Civilization, p. 302) writes thus concerning the customs in earliest Egypt: "The gods of the side which was victorious shared with it in the triumph and received a tithe of the spoil as the price of their help." Again (p. 706) in speaking of a king in relation to the gods among the ancient Chaldeans, he says: "As soon as he had triumphed by their command, he sought before all else to reward them amply for the assistance they had given. He poured a tithe of the spoils into the coffers of their treasury, he made over a part of the conquered country to their domain, he granted them a tale of the prisoners to cultivate their lands or to work at their buildings."

Prof. Maspero is writing of the earliest civilization which dates from 3000 to 4000 B. C., while Moses, it needs to be borne in mind, lived and wrote not more than 1500 years before Christ.

Prof. Hilprecht's splendid summary (Explorations in Bible Lands during the 19th Century, recently published) confirms this view. In giving account of Rassam's discoveries in the ruins of Abu Habba, the ancient Babylonian city of Sippara, he says (p. 275) the tablets discovered "make us acquainted with the duties and daily occupations of the different classes of temple officers and their large body of servants, with the ordinary tithes paid by the faithful, and with many other revenues accruing to the sanctuary from all kinds of gifts, from the lease of real estate, slaves, and animals, and from the sale of products from fields and stables. As tithes were frequently paid in kind, it became necessary to establish regular depots along the principal canals, where scribes stored and registered everything that came in. Among the goods thus received we notice vegetables, meat, and other perishable objects which the temple alone could not consume, and which, therefore, had to be sold or exchanged before they decayed or decreased in value. No wonder that apart from its distinct religious sphere the great temple of Shamash at Sippara in many respects resembled one of the great business firms of Babel or Nippur." He further says (p. 311), in speaking of some ancient tablets found in the ruins of ancient Nippur by the party of which he was a member, "they consisted of business documents referring to the registry of tithes, and to the administration of the temple property." These tablets discovered in 1888 proved to be a part of the great Temple Library discovered by Prof. Hilprecht in 1900. Many of them date back to the third millennium before Christ and some bear such names as that of the now famous author of the code of laws, Hammurabi; and others belong to the time as remote as that of Sargon, 3800 B. C.

In "Records of the Past" (edition of 1890, Vol. III., p. 96) we read "In a field of a tenth, he takes a tenth." "As for the tithe, he gives one part as tithe to the palace." Among the various kinds of divisions or land tenures, we find these two: "The division of a tenth," and "The division with a tithe." G. Bertin, the translator, says: "The work, as we know it from the fragment in the British Museum, is accompanied with a Babylonian translation of Sargon of Agade; and the fragments recovered are those of a Ninevite transcription made in the time of Asshurbanipal for his library." The tablets are divided into two columns, the left hand one giving the Akkadian and the right hand one the translation. The translator further says: "The tablet from which the above is a translation is of great importance as giving us information and particulars as to the system of land tenure and cultivation of land in the early Akkadian period." The date of this Sargon is now pretty well fixed at about 3800 B. C. This extensive system of land tenure being in vogue at that date argues that it had been in use in a less extensive form for a long time previous to the date of this publication.

The Pundit Dutt (Ancient India, Vol. II., p. 38), writing on "The Rationalistic Period, B. C. 1000-242," quotes Megasthenes of the Fourth Century B. C., who gives an account of the civil administration of a city during that period as saying: "Those who have charge of the city are divided into six bodies of five each." In enumerating the duties of each, he says: "The sixth and last class consists of those who collect the tenth of the prices of the articles sold."

Added to these references to China, India, Egypt, and Ancient Assyria and Babylonia, is the array of evidence commonly presented in writings on the tithe, including testimony from the Persians, Arabians, Phœnicians, Carthagenians and various other African communities, the ancient Britons, the Grecians and the Romans. One familiar instance from the Greeks will suffice for illustration.

In Xenophon's Anabasis, book V, chapter 3, we are told that "they divided the money raised from the sale of captives and of the tenth which they took out for Apollo and for the Ephesian Artemis (Diana of the Ephesians), the generals took each a part to keep for the gods." Referring to Xenophon's own home in Scillus, we read: "He made both an altar and a temple with the consecrated money; and also thereafter always collecting a tithe of the fruits of the season from the land, he offered sacrifice to the goddess; and all the citizens and neighboring men and women partook of the feast." A slab was set by the temple having the inscription, "The sacred place of Artemis. Let the one who has possession and enjoys the fruit thereof (i. e., of the estate) offer the tithe each year, and from the surplus repair the temple. If any one does not do this, it will be a care to the goddess," i. e., she will punish him as an offender.

We now come to the era of the Church Fathers. Here we will quote more at length because of the importance of this testimony to the minds of many who are dealing with this subject. It is understood that these witnesses are not to be regarded as final authorities to those of us who believe in the inspired revelation, but they are important and interesting because they reflect the practice of the Church when it was making its first great effort to preach the gospel to every creature and was making that effort, as is generally supposed, in use of methods sanctioned by the Apostles. The quotations, unless otherwise indicated, are from the edition of The Ante-Nicene, Nicene and Post-Nicene Fathers, published by the Christian Literature Co. of New York.

Clement (30-100 A. D.), who is generally agreed to be the one mentioned in Phil. 4:3, wrote a letter to the Corinthians, some think in 68, but the majority in 97 A. D. He says (Vol. I., p. 16), "These things therefore being manifest to us, and since we look into the depths of the divine knowledge, it behooves us to do all things in (their proper) order, which the Lord has commanded us to perform at stated times. He has enjoined offerings (to be presented) and service to be performed (to Him), and that not thoughtlessly or irregularly, but at the appointed times and hours. Where and by whom He desires these things to be done, He Himself has fixed by His own supreme will, in order that all things being piously done according to His good pleasure, may be acceptable unto Him. Those, therefore, who present their offerings at the appointed times, are accepted and blessed; for inasmuch as they follow the laws of the Lord, they sin not. For his own peculiar services are assigned to the high priest, and their own proper place is prescribed to the priests, and their own special ministrations devolve on the Levites. The layman is bound by the laws that pertain to laymen.

"Let every one of you, brethren, give thanks to God in his own order, living in all good conscience, with becoming gravity, and not going beyond the rule of the ministry prescribed to him. Not in every place, brethren, are the daily sacrifices offered, or the peace-offerings, or the sin-offerings and the trespass-offerings, but in Jerusalem only. And even there they are not offered in any place, but only at the altar before the temple, that which is offered being first carefully examined by the high priest and the ministers already mentioned. Those, therefore, who do anything beyond what is agreeable to His will, are punished with death. Ye see, brethren, that the greater the knowledge that has been vouchsafed to us, the greater also is the danger to which we are exposed."

In The Teaching of the Twelve Apostles (Vol. VII., p. 381), supposed to have been written about 120 A. D., we read: "But every true prophet that willeth to abide among you is worthy of support. So also a true teacher is himself worthy, as the workman, of his support. Every first-fruit, therefore, of the products of wine-press and threshing-floor, of oxen and of sheep, thou shalt take and give to the prophets, for they are your high priests. But if ye have not a prophet, give it to the poor. If thou makest a batch of dough, take the first-fruit and give according to the commandment. So also when thou openest a jar of wine or of oil, take the first-fruit and give it to the prophets; and of money (silver) and clothing and every possession, take the first-fruit, as it may seem good to thee, and give according to the commandment."

Justin Martyr (110-165) furnishes the following testimony (Vol. I., p. 167) when speaking of the changes that have taken place in the Christians. He says that, among other things, "we who valued above all things the acquisition of wealth and possessions, now bring what we have into a common stock, and communicate to every one in need." In describing a church service (186), he further says: "And they who are well-to-do, and willing, give what each thinks fit; and what is collected is deposited with the president, who succours the orphans and widows, and those who, through sickness or any other cause, are in want, and those who are in bonds, and the strangers sojourning among us, and in a word takes care of all who are in need."

Irenaeus (120-202) gives an exceedingly valuable discussion of the relation between the law and the gospel, in which (Vol. I., pp. 476, 477 and 478) he says: "As in the law, therefore, and in the Gospel (likewise), the first and greatest commandment is, to love the Lord God with the whole heart, and then there follows a commandment like to it, to love one's neighbor as one's self; the author of the law and the Gospel is shown to be one and the same. For the precepts of an absolutely perfect life, since they are the same in each Testament, have pointed out (to us) the same God, who certainly has promulgated particular laws adapted for each; but the more prominent and the greatest (commandments), without which salvation cannot (be attained), He has exhorted (us to observe) the same in both.... And that the Lord did not abrogate the natural (precepts) of the law, by which man is justified, which also those who were justified by faith, and who pleased God, did observe previous to the giving of the law, but that He extended and fulfilled them, is shown from His words." He then quotes examples from the Fifth Chapter of Matthew and speaks of the obedience of those who are freed from the bondage of the law, and adds: "And for this reason did the Lord, instead of that (commandment), 'Thou shalt not commit adultery,' forbid even concupiscence; and instead of that which runs thus, 'Thou shalt not kill,' He prohibited anger; and instead of the law enjoining the giving of tithes, (He told us) to share all our possessions with the poor; and not to love our neighbors only, but even our enemies; and not merely to be liberal givers and bestowers, but even that we should present a gratuitous gift to those who take away our goods.".... "Now all these (precepts), as I have already observed, were not (the injunctions) of one doing away with the law, but of one fulfilling, extending, and widening it among us; just as if one should say, that the more extensive operation of liberty implies that a more complete subjection and affection towards our Liberator had been implanted within us." In the light of these statements, we are to understand his words on pages 484 and 485. "And the class of oblations in general has not been set aside; for there were both oblations there (among the Jews), and there are oblations here (among the Christians). Sacrifices there were among the people; sacrifices there are, too, in the church; but the species alone has been changed, inasmuch as the offering is now made, not by slaves, but by freemen. For the Lord is (ever) one and the same; but the character of a servile oblation is peculiar (to itself), as is also that of freemen, in order that, by the very oblations, the indication of liberty may be set forth. For with Him there is nothing purposeless, nor without signification, nor without design. And for this reason they (the Jews) had indeed the tithes of their goods consecrated to Him, but those who have received liberty set aside all their possessions for the Lord's purposes, bestowing joyfully and freely not the less valuable portions of their property, since they have the hope of better things (hereafter); as that poor widow acted who cast all her living into the treasury of God."

Clement of Alexandria (153-217) writing about 200 A. D. says (Vol. II., p. 366), in discussing the source of the Greek virtues which he traces to the Jewish law, "Besides, the tithes of the fruits and of the flocks taught both piety toward the Deity, and not covetously to grasp everything, but to communicate gifts of kindness to one's neighbors. For it was from these, I reckon, and from the first-fruits that the priests were maintained. We now therefore understand that we are instructed in piety, and in liberality, and in justice, and in humanity by the law."

Tertullian (145-220), in describing the services of the Church, says (Vol. III., pp. 46, 47), "Though we have our treasure-chest, it is not made up of purchase-money, as of a religion that has its price. On the monthly day, if he likes, each puts in a small donation; but only if it be his pleasure, and only if he be able: for there is no compulsion; all is voluntary. These gifts are, as it were, piety's deposit fund. For they are not taken thence and spent on feasts, and drinking-bouts, and eating-houses, but to support and bury poor people, to supply the wants of boys and girls destitute of means and parents, and of old persons confined now to the house; such, too, as have suffered shipwreck; and if there happen to be any in the mines, or banished to the islands, or shut up in prisons, for nothing but their fidelity to the cause of God's Church, they become the nurslings of their confession. But it is mainly the deeds of a love so noble that lead many to put a brand upon us. See, they say, how they love one another, for themselves are animated by mutual hatred; how they are ready even to die for one another, for they themselves will sooner put to death.... One in mind and soul, we do not hesitate to share our earthly goods with one another." In answering the objection to their feasts as wicked and extravagant, he retorts, "The Salii cannot have their feast without going into debt; you must get the accountants to tell you what the tenths of Hercules and the sacrificial banquets cost."

Probably it will not be amiss to quote Tertullian on what he so aptly styles "the over-fed Christian," in view of the many appeals for money by catering to the stomach of the saints. On the subject of Fasting (Vol. IV., p. 113) he says, "With you 'love' shows its fervor in sauce-pans, 'faith' its warmth in kitchens, 'hope' its anchorage in waiters."

Origen (185-254) says (Vol. IV., p. 652), "Celsus would also have us to offer first-fruits to demons. But we would offer them to Him who said, 'let the earth bring forth grass, the herb yielding seed, and the fruit tree yielding fruit after his kind, whose seed is in itself upon the earth.' And to Him to whom we offer first-fruits we also send up our prayers." He is also quoted in Smith and Cheetham's Dictionary of Christian Antiquities as saying (Hom. XI., in Numeros), "How then is our righteousness abounding more than that of the Scribes and Pharisees, if they dare not taste the fruits of their land before they offer first-fruits to the priests, and tithes are separated for the Levites; whilst I, doing none of these things, so misuse the fruits of the earth that the priest knows nothing of them, the Levite is ignorant of them, the divine altar does not perceive them"?

Cyprian (200-258) in his treatise "On the Unity of the Church" (Vol. V., p. 429) states the condition of the Church in his time as follows: "But in us unanimity is diminished in proportion as liberality of working is decayed. Then they used to give for sale houses and estates; and that they might lay up for themselves treasures in heaven, presented to the apostles the price of them, to be distributed for the use of the poor. But now we do not even give the tenths from our patrimony; and while our Lord bids us sell, we rather buy and increase our store. Thus has the vigor of faith dwindled away among us; thus has the strength of believers grown weak."

The Apostolic Constitutions, connected in a literary way with The Teaching of the Twelve Apostles, belong, at least so far as the first six books are concerned, to the third century. Dr. Riddle says: "The first six books are the oldest; the seventh, in its present form, somewhat later, but, from its connection with the teaching, proven to contain matter of a very ancient date. The eighth book is of latest date. It now seems to be generally admitted that the entire work is not later than the fourth century, although the usual allowance must be made for textual changes, whether by accident or design."

Chapter 25 of book II. (Vol. VII., page 408) has the heading, "Of First-fruits and Tithes, and after what manner the Bishop is himself to partake of them, or to distribute them to others." The following sentences are culled out of this chapter: "Let him use those tenths and first-fruits, which are given according to the command of God, as a man of God; as also let him dispense in a right manner the free-will offerings which are brought in on account of the poor, to the orphans, the widows, the afflicted, and strangers in distress, as having that God for the examiner of his accounts who has committed the disposition to him.... The Levites, who attended upon the tabernacle, partook of those things that were offered to God by all the people.... You, therefore, O bishops, are to your people priests and Levites, ministering to the holy tabernacle, the holy Catholic Church.... As, therefore, you bear the weight, so have you a right to partake of the fruits before others, and to impart to those who are in want.... For those who attend upon the Church ought to be maintained by the Church, as being priests, Levites, presidents, and ministers of God."

Again in Chapter 35 (page 413) we read, "Now you ought to know, that although the Lord has delivered you from the additional bonds, and has brought you out of them to your refreshment, and does not permit you to sacrifice irrational creatures for sin-offerings, and purifications, and scape-goats, and continual washings and sprinklings, yet has He nowhere freed you from those oblations which you owe to the priests, nor from doing good to the poor." Other references will be found also on pages 471, 494, and among the Canons, page 500.

Jerome (345-420) writes in his letter to Nepotian (Vol. VI., Second Series) as follows: "I, if I am the portion of the Lord, and the line of His heritage, receive no portion among the remaining tribes; but, like the priest and the Levite, I live on the tithe, and serving the altar, am supported by its offerings.

Having food and raiment, I shall be content with these, and as a disciple of the Cross shall share its poverty."

Smith and Cheetham's Dictionary quotes Jerome as saying on Mal. 3:10, "What we have said of tithes and first-fruits which of old used to be given by the people to the priests and Levites, understand also in the case of the people of the Church, to whom it has been commanded to sell all they have and give to the poor and follow the Lord and Savior.... If we are unwilling to do this, at least let us imitate the rudimentary teaching of the Jews so as to give a part of the whole to the poor and pay the priests and Levites due honor. If any one shall not do this he is convicted of defrauding and cheating God."

The same authority quotes Ambrose (340-397) as saying (Sermon 34), "God has reserved the tenth part to Himself, and therefore it is not lawful for a man to retain what God has reserved for Himself. To thee He has given nine parts, for Himself He has reserved the tenth part, and if thou shalt not give to God the tenth part, God will take from thee the nine parts." Again in a sermon on Ascension Day, "A good Christian pays tithes yearly to be given to the poor."

From the same authority also, we get this from Augustine (354-430) who is quoted as saying (Hom. 48), "Our ancestors used to abound in wealth of every kind for this very reason that they used to give tithes, and pay the tax to Caesar. Now, on the contrary, because devotion to God has ceased, the drain of the treasury has increased. We have been unwilling to share the tithes with God, now the whole is taken away."

We quote further from Augustine (Vol. VI., First Series, page 367). "Let us give a certain portion of it. What portion? A tenth? The Scribes and Pharisees give tithes for whom Christ had not yet shed His blood. The Scribes and Pharisees give tithes; lest haply thou shouldst think thou art doing any great thing in breaking thy bread to the poor, and this is scarcely a thousandth part of thy means. And yet I am not finding fault with this; do even this. So hungry and thirsty am I, that I am glad even of these crumbs. But yet I cannot keep back what He who died for us said whilst He was alive, 'Except your righteousness shall exceed the righteousness of the Scribes and Pharisees, ye shall in no case enter into the kingdom of heaven.' The Scribes and Pharisees gave the tenth. How is it with you? Ask yourselves. Consider what you spend on mercy, what you reserve for luxury."

In commenting on Christ's saying in Luke 11:41, "Give alms, and behold all things are clean unto you," Augustine says (pages 435 and 436), "When He had spoken thus, doubtless they thought that they did give alms. And how did they give them? They tithed all they had, they took away a tenth of all their produce, and gave it. It is no easy matter to find a Christian who doth as much.".... Christ saith to them, "I know that ye do this, 'ye tithe mint and anise, cummin and rue,' but I am speaking of other alms: ye despise 'judgment and charity.'".... What is "in judgment"? Look back, and discover thyself; mislike thyself, pronounce judgment against thyself. And what is charity? "Love the Lord God with all thy heart, and with all thy soul, and with all thy mind; love thy neighbor as thyself: and thou hast done alms first to thine own soul, within thy conscience. Whereas if thou neglect this alms, give what thou wilt; reserve of thy goods not a tenth, but a half; give nine parts, and leave but one for thine own self: thou doest nothing, when thou dost not alms to thine own soul and art poor in thyself."

Once more we find Augustine saying (Vol. VIII., page 668), "Cut off some part of thy income; a tenth, if thou choosest, though that is but little. For it is said that the Pharisees gave a tenth.... He whose righteousness thou oughtest to exceed giveth a tenth: thou givest not even a thousandth. How wilt thou surpass him whom thou matchest not."

Chrysostom (347-407) preaches in much the same strain (Vol. XIII., page 69). "They gave tithes, and tithes again upon tithes for orphans, widows and strangers; whereas some one was saying to me in astonishment at another, 'Why, such a one gives tithes.' What a load of disgrace does this expression imply, since what was not a matter of wonder with the Jews has come to be so in the case of the Christians? If there was danger then in omitting tithes, think how great it must be now."

In preaching on Matt. 5:20, he says (Vol. X., pages 395, 396), "So that, though thou give alms, but not more than they, thou shalt not enter in. And how much did they bestow in alms? one may ask. For this very thing, I am minded to say now, that they who do not give may be roused to give, and they that give may not pride themselves, but may make increase of their gifts. What then did they give? A tenth of all their possessions, and again another tenth, and after this a third, so that they almost gave away the third part, for three-tenths put together make up this. And together with these, first-fruits, and first born, and other things besides, as, for instance, the offerings for sins, those for purification, those at feasts, those in the jubilee, those by the cancelling of debts, and the dismissal of servants, and the lendings that were clear of usury. But if he who gave the third part of his goods, or rather the half (for those being put together with these are the half), if he who is giving the half, achieves no great thing, he who doth not bestow so much as the tenth, of what shall he be worthy? With reason He said, 'There are few that be saved.'... For nothing else do I hear you saying everywhere, but such words as these: 'Such a one has bought so many acres of land; such a one is rich, he is building.' Why dost thou stare, O man, at what is without? Why dost thou look to others? If thou art minded to look to others, look to them that do their duty, to them that approve themselves, to them that carefully fulfill the law, not to those that have become offenders and are in dishonor."

Cassian (died about 432) in the First Conference of Abbott Thomas (Vol. XI., Second Series, p. 503, Ch. I.), makes record of the fact that certain young men, led by Thomas, were "eager to offer tithes and first-fruits of their substance" to Abbott John. This is said to be the first instance on record of payment of tithes to a monastery. In Ch. II. Abbott John thanks them for these gifts and refers to Prov. 3:9, 10 as promising a blessing for so doing. In chapters following, he speaks of tithes and other offerings as given by the Lord's commands and then instances the cases of Abraham, David, and other saints who went beyond the requirements of law. He argues that we who are under the gospel should sell all and give to the poor. "If even those who, faithfully offering tithes of their fruits, are obedient to the more ancient precepts of the Lord, cannot yet climb the heights of the gospel, you can see very clearly how far short of it those fall who do not even do this." While he holds that the law is no longer exacted, he makes this significant comment (p. 515). "But when the multitude of believers began day by day to decline from that apostolic fervor, and to look after their own wealth, and not to portion it out for the good of all the faithful in accordance with the arrangement of the Apostles, but having an eye to their own private expenses, tried not only to keep it, but actually to increase it, not content with following the example of Ananias and Sapphira, then it seemed good to all the priests that men who were hampered by world care, and almost ignorant, if I may say so, of abstinence and contrition, should be recalled to the pious duty by a fast canonically enjoined, and be constrained by the necessity of paying legal tithes, as this certainly would be good for the weak brethren and could not do any harm to the perfect who were living under the grace of the gospel and by their voluntary devotion going beyond the law." See also this same thought enlarged upon in Ch. 33.

Four bishops who were members of the Second Synod of Tours (567) issued a letter to the laity in which they assert that the tithe should be paid. (Hefele, Vol. I., p. 394). The Second Synod of Macon (585) enjoined afresh the law of the tithe under penalty of excommunication for refusal to observe it. This is the first official enactment that is considered authentic by those who are said to be authorities. From that time on its endorsement and enforcement became common and at length almost universal in the Church. The first Christian emperors assigned land and other property to ministers for their support, but enacted no law respecting the tithe. The first legal enactment was made by Charlemagne, king of the Franks, 768-800, and Roman emperor, 800-814. His Capitularies established its practice in the Roman empire, and thence it spread to other lands. Offa, king of Mercia, introduced the tithe system into England about the close of the eighth century, and

Ethelwulf in the ninth century, or according to Clarke (History of Tithes), Athelstan 927, made it a law for the whole English realm. To what the tithe was to be devoted was optional until Innocent III., through the Archbishop of Canterbury, 1200, issued a decretal requiring tithes to be paid to the clergy of the parish to which the payee belonged, which decree Clarke says was inoperative until reissued by the General Council of Lateran, 1215, when the parson was finally given the parochial right to the tithes. The tithe was introduced into Portugal and Denmark in the eleventh century, into Sweden in the thirteenth, and soon became a general law of Christendom.

The Roman secular law provided that any one who obtained a part of the public land in a conquered country should pay to the state a tenth of the revenue he derived from its rent, and this system was usually transferred to the colonies settled on the soil. When the church tithe came into prominence there arose two kinds, secular and ecclesiastical tithes, which to a greater or less extent have been associated and commingled in almost every civilization from the earliest times. It would be impossible, were it deemed necessary, to state in a brief limit the minutiæ of this complicated tithe system. It was not abolished by the Reformation. Luther and Calvin believed in tithing for the support of the Church. It may be worth while to quote from the First Book of Discipline, which Knox heartily approved. One section runs as follows: "The sums able to sustain the forenamed persons, and to furnish all things appertaining to the preservation of good order and policy within the Kirk, must be lifted of tenths, the tenth sheaf of all sorts of corn, hay, hemp and lint: tenth fish, tenth calf, tenth lamb, tenth wool, tenth foal, tenth cheese. And because that we know that the tenth reasonably taken, as is before expressed, will not suffice to discharge the former necessity" it directs other gifts and rents. These Reformers, however, felt the burden of the enforced tithe and the movement grew apace to remove it. It was abolished in France in 1789. Other countries where any law obtains, have largely commuted it to a fixed annual sum of money, after the system in vogue in England to-day. Enlightened Christendom is rightfully rebelling against this enforced tribute and is looking for a more spontaneous support.

LINES OF ARGUMENT.

There are certain conclusions, it seems to me, which may safely be drawn from this brief summary of the evidence now before us. First: THE TITHE IS A UNIVERSAL PRINCIPLE, NOT A LEVITICAL INSTITUTION.

It seems peculiar to one who has studied the subject in the light of the new data which is now being brought to light so abundantly, that one should be so regularly confronted with the assertion that the tithe is a Levitical institution. It is stranger still that so many ministers continue to assert this as a fact, when the unanimous testimony of such men as Prof. Sayce, Prof. Maspero, Dr. Hilprecht and others of their standing can easily be gathered to the contrary. They all assert that no matter how old the civilization there is always abundant evidence of proportionate giving to the gods and almost invariably the tenth. The only apparent exception is in the Laws of Manu of Ancient India, wherein we find one-tenth, one-eighth, and one-sixth specified as the tribute to the king who doubtless saw to it that one-sixth became general in India. It is likely that if we had the most ancient laws we would find that the one-tenth prevailed, even in India.

Just as I had reached this stage in writing, there came to my notice a communication from Rev. Henry Lansdell, D. D., London, England, calling attention to his investigations in the same line, which abundantly confirm the statements made. He gives two personal incidents which I deem worthy of record here. "The Rev. J. E. Padfield, a missionary of my acquaintance, whose station at Musulipatam I visited in 1890, took the pains to inquire systematically and in detail over his large district, of every native Christian family in each congregation, as to how much heathen in their own social position would pay, or what would have been the amount of their own religious offerings had they continued to be heathens. This was done with a view to comparison with what they gave for Christian religious purposes of every kind. As a result of that inquiry it was stated that the high caste Brahmins had been wont to spend for religious purposes the equivalent of a month's income per annum; the lower castes, such as farmers, cultivators, and coolies spending less: but speaking of these particular Christians as a whole it appeared that whilst they were heathen they had to expend upon religious observances not less than one-thirteenth of their net incomes."

Once more: when prosecuting my studies one day at the British Museum, I was accosted by a well-educated young Sikh, who came from Amritsar, and was brother, or near relative, of the chief priest of the Golden Temple, which I remember to have visited. Upon my asking for any information he could give relative to the subject I was studying, he said that, in the time of Baba Aryan Sodhi, the fifth Sikh Guru (or teacher), the people gave a tenth part of their incomes for religious purposes; but that in the present day, good Sikhs give about one-twentieth, though the proportion varies. These examples confirm what I have learned from missionaries as to the present status of the subject in India, and largely also in many other countries. The latter instance tends to prove that at times in the earlier history of India the tithe has prevailed, which is the point with which we are at present concerned.

Seeing that the tithe has been so universal, it may be of interest to inquire why it should have been so universal. It matters little whether you take the portion offered to the gods or the tribute to the kings as the Sons of Heaven and representatives of the gods, why should we find in all these ancient civilizations one-tenth as the universal offering? Why should not all have had one-sixth as in India at one time? It surely cannot be ascribed to the inherent generosity of the priests and rulers. Seven is also a sacred number. Why did they not require one-seventh?

The tithe finds an interesting parallel in sacrifice with which it is closely connected. For when one is commanded to sacrifice, the minimum at least must be set to his sacrifice. Sacrifice, I believe, was a divine institution given to our first parents in Eden. Most likely the tithe is seen, in germ at least, in the offerings of Cain and Abel. The Council of Seville viewed Cain's sin as one of covetousness in withholding a portion of the tithe or part that God required. The Septuagint reading of Gen. 4:7, which the early Church Fathers seem invariably to adopt, and a literal translation of Heb. 11:4 point to this view. Personally I like to translate the latter "more of a sacrifice" which is simple and includes both the idea of quantity and that of quality and spirit. Wickliffe translated it "a much more sacrifice." Westcott maintains that this is correct. The critical scholars generally admit that such is the natural rendering, but claim not to be able to see why such a thing should be said. Covetousness played so prominent a part in the parent's fall, why should it not in the son's sin, seeing that it is one of the most persistent of the Satan brood? Dr. John Brown, in his Commentary on Hebrews, Vol. II., page 41, quotes another who says: "It is easy to be demonstrated that sacrifices owe their original to the will and appointment of God. The Apostle says, as Moses said before him, that Abel's sacrifice was acceptable to God. But it would not have been acceptable if it had not been of divine institution, according to that plain, obvious and eternal maxim of all true religion, Christian, Mosaic, and natural, 'In vain do they worship God, teaching for doctrines the commandments of men,' Mark 7:7. If there be any truth in this maxim, Abel would have worshipped God in vain, and God would have had no respect to his offering, if his sacrifice had been merely a commandment of his father Adam, or an invention of his own. The divine acceptance, therefore, is a demonstration of a divine institution."

This line of argument is almost unanimously accepted among Christian scholars as an adequate basis for the belief that sacrifice was a divine institution. Why is it not fully as applicable to tithing? It is not stated in Scripture, prior to the giving of the Mosaic law, that either is a divine institution. But if "divine acceptance is a demonstration of a divine institution," the tithe has as clear a demonstration of its origin as has sacrifice. Now and then in Scripture the whole business of sacrifice is spoken of in a deprecating way. Cf. Heb. 10. Such is not the case in respect to the tithe, unless Amos 4:4 be so taken.

But whatever view one may take of the origin of the tithe, there can be no reason for the claim that it is a Jewish institution. It is true that there are some people who seem to think that Adam was the first Jew and that everything from Adam to Christ was Jewish. In the very region whence came Abraham, the first Jew, the tithe was in force as early as 3800 B. C., which is nearly 2000 years before there was a Jew. It was as well defined in Babylonia at that period as it was in Judea in the time of Moses and would much better be called Babylonian than Jewish.[B]

In conclusion, we may reiterate the words of Dr. Kennicott. "Whatever custom has prevailed over the world, among nations the most opposite in polity and customs in general, nations not united by commerce or communication (when that custom has nothing in nature or the reason of things to give it birth, and establish to itself such a currency), must be derived from some revelation, which revelation may in certain places have been forgotten, though the custom introduced by and founded on such a revelation still continued; and further, this revelation must have been antecedent to the dispersion at Babel, when all mankind, being but one nation and living together in the form of one large family, were of one language and governed by the same laws and customs." With sacrifice, the tithe went abroad over the face of the whole earth and survived long after its origin was forgotten. If "in the annals of all times none are found which did not pay tithes" among the nations of the past, either as an offering to the gods or as a tribute to the rulers, the evidence certainly warrants the conclusion that "offerings of at least one-tenth to God, was a primeval appointment not for the Jews, but for all nations."

Second: ALTHOUGH UNIVERSAL IT WAS INCORPORATED INTO AND MADE THE BASIS OF THE MOSAIC SYSTEM OF TITHES.

In the Mosaic system there was a general tithe, conforming in every feature to this universal tithe. Then there was a second tithe, of national significance only, used as material for a feast at a designated place the first and second year. But the third year it was to be eaten at home, the poor sharing in the feast. This is the best view, I think, of what some call the third tithe. Hence every Jew offered two-tenths each year besides the first-fruits and all other offerings free-will and required. Counting the first-fruits at from one-thirtieth to one-sixtieth (as rabbis tell us they were estimated) the Jew must needs give about twenty-five per cent of all his yearly income. Chrysostom figures it at a third to a half, but the probability is that he has it too high. Those of us who speak on the tithe are often accused of trying to put the Church back on the Jewish basis, which is another of those foolish things that even some fairly intelligent people seem to never tire of saying, no matter how little sense there is in them. To reach a Jewish basis, the average Christian would have to give at least ten times what he is now giving, not merely one-tenth of his income. Let us get up to the heathen standard, before we worry too much about being Judaized.

Third: BEING UNIVERSAL THE PRINCIPLE OF THE TITHE IS NOT TO BE COUNTED AS ABROGATED WHEN THE OLD TESTAMENT ECONOMY ENDED, UNLESS IT BE SO STATED OR AT LEAST BY FAIR INFERENCE BE IMPLIED.

It certainly is not stated anywhere in the New Testament that the tenth is no longer the Lord's. Neither can any fair inference be drawn showing that it is no longer holy to the Lord. The two incidents cited, it is true, contain rebukes to the Pharisees who were tithers, but the tithing is not condemned any more than is prayer or fasting. It is the manner, not the principle, that is condemned. On the contrary, tithing is emphatically commended. For the Savior says, "These ought ye to have done and not to have left the other undone." I am well aware that it is the reply of many that Christ merely commended their doing what was a plain duty under the Mosaic law, but that he in no way implies that such a duty was binding on others. Granting that the first statement is an assumption, then we have it answered by another assumption, with the result that the whole statement of Christ is of no weight in the matter. Christ did not always fall in with the teachings of the Mosaic system, as for example in the matter of granting divorce. If He had wanted to do away with the tithe, certainly He could have said so, as clearly as He did in matters of divorce. He does not here, or elsewhere, offer any substitute for this universal standard, and He spoke often on the subject of money and of covetousness. One verse in every four in the gospels by Matthew, Mark, and Luke have to do with these subjects, and one verse in every six in the whole New Testament. Certainly if a new standard were to be revealed, there is abundance of opportunity.

The objection may be stated here that sacrifice was likewise universal. True enough, but we have fulfillment of all its obligations and typical significance in the perfect sacrifice, "The Lamb of God which taketh away the sin of the world," "Our High Priest who needeth not daily like those high priests who offer up sacrifices, first for his own sin and then for the sins of the people. For this he did once for all when he offered up himself."

I have also met this objection. Circumcision and polygamy were universal, and your argument would establish them. In the first place circumcision was never universal, and even if it had been, we have numerous statements in the New Testament denying its further claim and a seal of the covenant, as I believe, clearly revealed which was to supersede it. As to polygamy, it may be safely affirmed that it never was divinely commanded, it is contrary to a definite law of God, announced to our first parents, and reaffirmed in the New Testament.

With sacrifice all the rites of ceremonial significance and the retinue of priests and Levites which administered them came to an end. All moral obligations, however, were not abolished, but many of them were more strictly interpreted. The Sermon on the Mount reveals a higher conception of moral obligation and requires a purer motive than any precept of the Old Testament. The laws of home relationship are made more binding. The bill of divorcement is swept away and only the great principle recognized, namely, faithlessness to the universal law, "Thou shalt not commit adultery." Even in the case of ritual offering this is true. Take an example. While incense is abolished, that which is symbolized, the great heart beat of humanity which we call prayer, is not abolished but is enlarged to a precept of exceeding broad scope, "Pray without ceasing."

Now we demand some word of fair implication at least, or some example to show that the universal obligation of the tithe has been set aside in the general shaking up of the earth. It was not removed as being one of "the things that are made," but, as I believe, it remains as one of "the things which cannot be shaken." This statement is borne out by the evidence afforded from its history. "These thing ought ye to have done" is a word that justifies our conclusion.

Fourth: NOT BEING ABROGATED WHEN THE OLD TESTAMENT ECONOMY ENDED, IT IS UNIVERSALLY BINDING IN THE NEW TESTAMENT DISPENSATION.

Notwithstanding all that has been written to the contrary, I am firmly persuaded that this was recognized by the early Church. The quotations cited are abundantly sufficient to prove this statement, if fairly interpreted. And this leads me to enter a protest against the unfair presentation of this evidence on the part of many writers. This can be illustrated by the case of Irenaeus who is invariably, so far as I have seen, set down as on the side of the abrogation of the law of the tithe, because he said in one place as quoted on page 17 "instead of the law enjoining the giving of tithes, (He told us) to share all our possessions with the poor." Certainly nothing could be found, nor is found, more explicit than that statement. Yet any one who reads the whole context will see that Irenaeus is contending for just the opposite thing. He classes the tithe, not with the ceremonial things, but with the natural precepts, by which he means the moral law as is clearly shown. To argue that Irenaeus is abrogating the tithe, is to argue that he is doing away with the law of adultery and murder, for he mentions them in exactly the same language. The same thing would be true of the commandment to love our neighbors. But why should we debate this point when Irenaeus distinctly says, "all these precepts, as I have already observed, were not (the injunctions) of one doing away with the law, but of one fulfilling, extending, and widening it among us."

Now I should like to know how it comes that all these learned men who speak so surely of Irenaeus have always neglected to quote Irenaeus as to what he really meant? Personally, I am willing to stake the whole case on Irenaeus. For I do not know a better presentation of the whole question than he makes. When he includes tithing under the head of the moral precepts of the law and then says emphatically "that the Lord did not abrogate the natural (precepts) of the law," I am sure that he stated the whole truth in respect to this subject. That he enlarged their scope and raised the maximum of moral requirement, he rightly affirms. When that is understood there is no more room for debate.

But why such dreadful alarm over this tithe law? Why, for example, should the writer in Smith and Cheetham's Dictionary try to minimize all this testimony of the Father's? He is anxious to prove that "the evidence belonging to this period would seem to show that payment of tithe was first regarded as a duty soon after A. D. 350. By that time the idea generally prevailed that the priest of the Christian Church had succeeded to the office of the Levitical priests, and consequently to their rights and privileges." His bogy comes to light in the following: "Cyprian (Epist. 1:9, Ed. Erasmus, 66 Pamel.) writes to dissuade a presbyter from accepting the position of guardian on the ground that the clergy are separated from all secular business. The tribe of Levi had no inheritance but was supported by tithes, that they might devote themselves entirely to divine service; 'the same plan and form is now preserved in regard to the clergy' that they may not be diverted from their sacred duties, but 'receiving as it were tithes may not depart from the altar.' Here the phrase tanquam decimas is decisive against the payment of tithe as a fixed legal due, for decimae paid as legal dues could not be tanquam decimae. There is analogy, not identity in the method of support." The word "legal" is the key to all this twisting and trembling. This will be explained, perhaps, when we recall that he is an Englishman, and comes of a race that has suffered much from enforced tithing. Uhlhorn's Christian Charity in the Ancient Church is marred by the same tremendous anxiety to kill off any hope of this legal monster ever getting loose again. Hence it seems that it is now time to say that the tithe never was in Bible times, the legal monster that it afterward became. Under Old Testament teaching and practice, the tithe was voluntary. No hand of force was used to collect it, but as in the time of Hezekiah, the people brought in the tithes willingly and abundantly. It was a moral precept, enforced by appeals to the conscience. Hezekiah does not reckon on the tithes in a way that indicates that he would compel them to be brought in, but expresses his gratitude when he finds that so much was brought in by the people. The appeal of Malachi to the nation that had robbed God is a moral appeal and is based upon the same thought that we find in all such appeals of Scripture. That the Pharisees by their traditions had reduced it to a burdensome legal requirement need not be questioned. So did they weigh down every moral precept that the Lord ever laid upon the conscience of men. The advocacy of the tithe in this country is always on the voluntary basis, so far as I know. I feel that it would be a calamity were it put on any other basis, and I know that all who are working in this line, so far as I have become acquainted with their work, have the same feeling. What we believe is that this is God's standard of giving, a minimum below which one cannot fall and be entitled to a claim on God's rich promises of blessing to those who give money for His work. The maximum claim is the one of which the Fathers so often speak. Matt. 19:21. "Sell that thou hast, and give to the poor, and thou shalt have treasure in heaven." Between these two claims love finds its field of operation and its measure of perfectness. This is our view and the view which I think prevailed in the early Church.

Clement's Letter to the Corinthians, the nearest writing to the inspired books of the New Testament, says: "Those who present their offerings at the appointed times are blessed; for inasmuch as they follow the laws of the Lord they sin not." (See page 14.) The context clearly shows that he has in mind the laws governing the offerings to the priests and Levites. The Teaching speaks of "giving according to the commandment," which must mean the Levitical commandment, or one similar to it. Justin Martyr first says that they put what they "have into a common stock" and later says "they who are well-to-do and willing, give what each thinks fit," and in both cases seems to intimate that what is contributed is given to the dependent. (See page 16.) His last instance of giving as each one thinks fit, may be a description applicable to those who sought to follow the law of the free-will offering which is laid down in Deut. 16:10, 17, and reaffirmed by the Apostle in I Cor. 16:2. A special contribution to the poor would be made now on the same basis in any of our churches and does not touch the subject of the regular support of the Church. Yet many ministers who ought to know better, insist on saying that this is the New Testament law of giving. It is most decidedly not a New Testament, but an Old Testament law, confirmed by the New

Testament, and by common sense apart from any question of Scripture authority.

If Justin meant to affirm that this regulation was in force, well and good. But if he meant to say, as some would have us believe, that the Church had thus early gotten on the basis of every man doing exactly as he pleased, then all we have to say is that from our modern experience with that sort of teaching, we cannot commend his judgment or the practice of the Church of which he was a part, for no such principle, ever had, or ever can have, the sanction of God. Again how this can be reconciled with the statement that they have put all into the common stock is more than I can see. How could men be well-to-do who had sold all and put it into the hands of others? It may be for convenience of his argument that he describes in the first case what some few have done, perhaps himself among the number, and that in the Church service, he is telling of either the observance of the rule of the free-will offering, or else is letting us into a state of anarchy respecting the proper teaching on the subject of giving, which led to the difficulties of the later centuries. The same comment may be made on the statements of Tertullian. It will be noted that he does not tell how the aggressive work of the Church is to be supported, but only of what is secured for what we commonly call charitable purposes.

It may be that the reason we begin to hear of shortcomings in giving as early as in the time of Origen and Cyprian, is that this every-man-do-as-he-thinks-fit teaching is bearing its legitimate fruit and that now there must be some heroic measures taken to offset its fatal influence. From what these witnesses tell us, the Church of the third century was reaping the fruit of some erroneous teaching and practice in respect to the giving of money. From that time on the call is to a recognition of duty, as all the extracts go to show. The gift of the maximum had been made by the few. The many had followed their own will and the result was disastrous to the Church, and we are not surprised that the later writings abound in appeals to the people to meet even the minimum demands of the tithe, if they ever expected to exceed the righteousness of the Scribes and Pharisees.

But it is to be noted that only Justin Martyr and Tertullian seem to endorse a hit and miss plan of giving. With these exceptions, the Fathers agree that the laborers in the kingdom of Christ take the place of the ministers of the Mosaic period, and deserve to be as well supported, according to the teaching of Christ in Matt. 10:10 and Luke 10:7, enforced by that of Paul in I Cor. 9:7-11 and I Tim. 5:18. And here it may be said in passing, that Paul justifies his plea for support in the work of the Gospel by—"Saith not the law the same also?" If the law confirms the justice of the laborer's claim under the Gospel, is it such a perversion of the spirit of the Gospel to urge that one do not fall short of a plain requirement of that same law? This identification of the teachers of both dispensations and of the method of their support is not a later growth, as the Smith and Cheetham's writer would have us believe, but is found in the very earliest writings. It is quite likely that different practices prevailed at different times and in different places in the Church. But it is to be borne in mind that with the two exceptions named, the testimony is for meeting God's requirement, whether it be that the requirement was considered to be the whole or the tithe, and that there is no approval given to the do-as-you-please plan in matters of conduct.

Here I think it in place to repeat some things said in Tithe Conferences at Winona and elsewhere during the past year in regard to one of the most persistent and misguided of all the objections with which we are confronted. It is urged that the New Testament bases all action on love and that one must give according to his love and that this is the only Christian standard of life and service. This is confusion much confounded. It is a fixed principle of ethics that men cannot be a law to themselves and civilization be preserved and conduct properly regulated. Though good men may fail to see it, this method of giving according to the measure of one's love is, at the bottom, anarchy pure and simple. Every man is left to determine what he shall do according to the impulse of the moment and without any regard to a fixed standard of right. Such a principle cannot be tolerated in social life. There is a standard of law which makes the right for one the right for all and to set this aside in any case is to invite trouble. In all human conduct, a fixed standard, apart from men, must be the basis of right. It must be invariable and must obtain in one life as much as in another. Hence this high-sounding plea for love as the basis of all action is pure anarchy in Christian guise. Lawless grace is as loveless as lawless humanity. License claimed on account of standing under grace, though put on a heavenly plane, is hell-born just the same. License means anarchy, and anarchy is devilish though concerned with the holiest of occupations. To make love a standard of action is to confuse a motive and a standard. Love is variable, not the same in any two individuals, and not the same in any individual at different times.

Has love no place in God's scheme? Certainly it has, and a very large place at that. God's plan does not limit love in its maximum which is all "that thou hast." But what we contend is that God does have a minimum standard below which one cannot fall and claim to have the love of Christ constraining him. Love fulfills law, doesn't abrogate it as so many seem to think. The law says, Remember the Sabbath day to keep it holy. Love says, I will make that day and every day holy unto the Lord, but does not say, I will do away with the law altogether as to that which God has made the minimum requirement of the race. Love may go beyond the law's requirement, but will not fall below it. Love does not and cannot repeal law, but obeys it and furnishes the only true motive to obedience. Grace alters and exalts the motive but cannot free from the obligations of law.

A little clear thinking at this point would do much to set many people right on this question and on many other questions of Christian life. The large amount of Pharisaical floundering and pietistic mouthing with which the Church is persecuted on this behalf is not creditable to our intelligence or to our Christianity. So simple and fundamental is this point both from the standpoint of ethics and of religion that it seems strange that sane men should ever call it in question. But men were troubled with it when Paul wrote his letter to the Romans and are still troubled with it and strangest of all quote Paul's words which were written to set people straight on this matter as the justification of the very thing he was trying to correct. To me this is one of the most peculiar perversions of Scripture which has ever arisen in the history of the Church. That the epistle to the Romans which has for its key word righteousness (which I think means rightness according to God's standard and which can have no other satisfactory meaning), should be taken as the authority for Antinomianism which practically annihilates law is certainly a singular proof of the fact that some people have the logical faculty in a very rudimentary state. It seems to me that we ought to be able to see that if God's standard of right is abrogated, then nothing can control a man's life but his own promptings. What is a law but God's standard of right in respect to that particular line of conduct to which it applies? What is the abrogation of law but the doing away with God's standard and the substitution of a human standard? We have become so afraid of the charge of legalism that we have swung far to the side of anarchy, and, as between the two, legalism is the least to be feared, as bad as it is. Plain speech is needed for we must not palliate the consequences of such teaching. Paul meant well as a persecutor, but Paul the preacher greatly deplored his course of action in such a rôle. Men may think they are doing God and humanity service by such advocacy, but to me it is the devil's work and makes for lawlessness which is sin and which when finished brings forth death. Lawlessness abounds in teaching of school and Church and is it any wonder that we stand horrified at some of its outbreaks in our very midst? Herein I find a most urgent call to advocate the right as God has indicated it in respect to giving as well as to any other of the lines of conduct which go to make up a well-rounded life.

Giving is not left to the emotions of men, no matter how pure and holy they may seem to be. Giving is to be according to God's measure or requirement. To this it seems we ought all to agree. Has God a measure? If so, what is it and how does it operate? Some of us think that He has and that it is fixed and invariable, the same always and for all. Why should he not have? Honest people of business ability do not sell wheat by whim, potatoes for appearance sake, or calico by hysterics. Produce is measured by well-defined standards and disposed of in due regard to and careful consideration of the principles of economic distribution. Why be so careless in respect to moral conduct? Ethical principles ought to be, and I believe are more clearly defined than are economic principles. What is the rule, what the standard, are the first questions concerning any moral act. When this is known the character of the act is easily determined. Every grace or fruit of the spirit is to be tested by this vital inquiry. Faith, the first-fruit, has a unit of measure. Belief unto salvation is the minimum of faith. Beyond that faith may reach to heights that seem to have no limit. But it must measure up to that minimum, or fail to merit the name of faith. Love the final-fruit, as we sometimes say, has its unit, namely, the gift of self. No gift without the giver, no love without the lover. These minimum requirements are agreed upon by all teachers of the gospel of redemption from sin through the blood of Jesus Christ. No one supposes for a moment that such teaching involves the idea that faith and love shall never go beyond this minimum. They must go on to perfection.

This brings us to answer that provoking misrepresentation of the position of tithers which claims that men ought to give more than the tithe and that love to Christ should lead to the consecration of all to Him. I do not know of any tither who feels that the tenth is all that he ought to give. Most pastors know that if extra money is wanted, the tithers are not the last to respond. Further, I have never heard such doctrine advocated by any tither. We persistently say that we are dealing with the minimum, not with the maximum, not with the outgoings of hearts full of love to Christ, but with those who are robbing God of even His minimum and are thus guilty of the awful crime of covetousness, which the New Testament places among the vilest of crimes and says that it will shut out of the kingdom. The fifth chapter of I Corinthians clearly teaches that the covetous brother is to be shut out of the fellowship of Christians, even in this life. How does the treatment of the rich man by many churches and communities square with this plain teaching? The early Fathers were very faithful in teaching concerning the crime of covetousness, following in the footsteps of the Apostles and of Christ Himself. How about the minister who considers himself above the business of mentioning money matters to the congregation? This rank Phariseeism needs to be driven out of the minds of ministers and theological teachers who train ministers. If they spoke on this subject as often as Christ did, they would need to preach on it about once a month. Mr. Kane's experience wherein after three heroic efforts, he only succeeded in finding theological professors and students in about half the seminaries in this country and Canada who were willing to receive literature which he offered to furnish gratis, speaks of an awful perversion of Scripture teaching on this subject and a failure to grasp the vital questions of Christian life which it touches. Is it any wonder that there is a constant "drain of the treasury" as Augustine said?

Wrestle with it as we may, the consecrate-all-to-the-Lord and all such plans, have proved a dismal failure in respect to bringing "meat" into God's house, and the crying need of the hour is money to send workers into all the world to preach the gospel. Whatever be your scheme for getting the money, you know, brother pastor and fellow-workers, that the great hindrance to enlargement of the Church's work is money to meet necessary expenditures. Some one always bobs up with the mystical dictum that it is prayer, or consecration, or something to that effect. But that is only beating the Devil around the bush. For the promised result of the prayer, or the consecration, or whatever one may suggest, is that money will be forthcoming. So after all it is money that must be gotten, by whatsoever means one may employ.

The giving of all to the Lord is the only New Testament method which is offered us as an alternative. I am free to say that it has failed to meet the case not only in our age, and in the age of the Fathers who rang the changes on it, but I am persuaded also that it did not meet the case in the days of the Apostles. It must always be remembered that it was voluntary, as Peter said to Ananias, and though voluntary, it did not fail to present difficulties very early in the history of the Church, as the sixth chapter of Acts shows. Again it should be remembered that the very fact that Paul was instructed to call for a collection for the poor saints in Jerusalem proves two things at least. That the needs of the Church were not met by this voluntary communism, and that this communism had not been adopted elsewhere to any great extent, else the appeal to people to lay aside for this free-will offering as God had prospered them would have been a piece of pious nonsense.

The Jewish Encyclopedia (Vol. III., p. 668) gives an interesting bit of evidence as to the effect of this movement. We read that "against the tendency prevailing in Essene and Christian circles to sell all one had and 'give to the poor' in order to have 'treasure in heaven' (Matt. 19:21), the rabbis at the Synod in Usha ordained that 'no one should give away more than the fifth of his fortune lest from independence he may lapse into a state of dependence'" (Ket. 50 a). While the evil effect of anything Christian is apt to be overstated by these Jewish writers, still may it not be that here we have proof that communism, tried under the most favorable circumstances, as it certainly was under the early Church management, fails to meet the case, and that Christ's saying, "The poor always ye have with you," was still true and even more emphasized under this method of social life? The fact seems to stand out even on the pages of the book of Acts with special emphasis that such a method, with the very best management, does not take away the problem of the dependent, but really intensifies it.

The Apostle Paul seems to have had to deal with this tendency toward abuse of charity and in doing so laid down some very fundamental propositions to which the Church ought always to give heed. "For even when we were with you, this we commanded you, that if any would not work, neither should he eat. For we hear that there are some which walk among you disorderly, working not at all, but are busybodies. Now them that are such we command and exhort by our Lord Jesus Christ, that with quietness they work, and eat their own bread." II Thess. 3:10-12. "If any provide not for his own, and specially for those of his own house, he hath denied the faith, and is worse than an infidel." I Tim. 5:8. These positive teachings certainly argue that Paul did not approve of the communistic plan, for how could one eat his own bread or provide for his own household, if he had put all into the common fund? In short, Paul, as the great organizer of the Church, does not give a single hint that he approved of such a method. All his statements are emphatic on the other side. Even his own custom of working for his living argues his disapproval of the communistic idea. This should be borne in mind by those who are so sure that Christian Socialism as they choose to call it, will solve all the problems respecting the poor. Personally, I believe that Paul's method is the better one and will come nearer than any other to the solution.

The question is often asked, why does not the New Testament say more about the tithe, if it is still the universal law? The answer to this has usually been, that all the peoples to whom the apostles preached had been accustomed to give at least a tenth for religious purposes and they found no particular need to lay emphasis upon what was a universal practice. Also that the enthusiastic support through voluntary communism and other large free-will offerings made it unnecessary for them to dwell upon it. These answers have weight and might be counted sufficient, if it were not that they seem to assume that the New Testament is silent on this great question. Attention has been called to Christ's commendation of the tithing principle and to Paul's appeal to the law. But it seems to me that not enough is made of the treatment of this subject in the one book in which we would naturally expect it, that is, in the book of Hebrews. The writer was trying to convince these Hebrews of the incomparably superior character of Christ and His priesthood to that to which they were so attached. We would naturally suppose that here, if anywhere, we would have some discussion of the tribute to this great High Priest and that is just what we have in the seventh chapter.

Rev. Henry Constable (Gold or the Gospel) has well said, "The Levitical priesthood, by the command of God, received tithes of their people. It follows as certainly that Melchizedek had the same claim to a tenth from Abraham which they had from the Jews, i. e., a divine command. For, surely, if a tenth were Levi's right by divine ordinance, while Melchizedek had no such right at all, he is in this respect inferior to Levi, and Paul's argument from his reception of a tenth from Abraham an inconclusive one." Why, too, if Christ does not have such a right and does not receive the tithe is He not in that respect at least inferior to Levi?

Again, we quote Dr. John Owen. "When Abraham himself gave tithes to Melchizedek, he did it not in his own name only, but in the name of himself, and his whole posterity." He argues the significance of the act as follows. Abram was called to be "the foundation of a new church;" he "had now received the promise" not only for himself, but for "all his seed in him," and whatever he "did in obedience unto God, he did undertake in it for his posterity." Wherefore "Abraham, in this solemn address unto God by Melchizedek the type of Christ, wherein he expressed his covenant obedience unto him, was the representative of all his posterity and in particular of Levi and all the priest that descended from him. And having now received the whole land, by virtue of a covenant, in behalf of his posterity, that it should be theirs, though he himself had never possession of it nor in it, he doth in the name of his posterity, and as their representative, give the tenth unto God by Melchizedek, as the chief rent which God forever reserved unto himself, upon the grant." This is a remarkable argument from one who earlier in his comments rather hesitatingly tries to break the force of the tithe argument in general, largely, it is evident, because of the misuse of it under the monstrous enforced system of his day. However, if we, as Paul contends in Galatians, are children of faithful Abraham, and "there are not two churches, but two states of the same church" as Dr. Owen puts it, then either Scripture contradicts itself, or we prove false to our covenant relationship and dishonor Christ when we do not do homage to Him in person, as our father Abraham did in type in the paying of tithes. I see no escape from this alternative.

Calvin is the only commentator, so far as I have seen, that has given a consistent interpretation to the 8th verse. He says, "For he thus reasons— those to whom the Law assigns tithes are dying men; by which it was indicated that the priesthood would some time be abrogated, as their life came to an end: but the Scripture makes no mention of the death of Melchizedek, when it relates that tithes were paid to him, so the authority of his priesthood is limited by no time, but on the contrary, there is given an indication of perpetuity. But this is added for this purpose, lest a posterior law, as it is usual, should seem to take away from the authority of the former law. For it might have been otherwise objected and said, that the right which Melchizedek formerly possessed is now void and null, because God had introduced another law by Moses, by which He transferred the right to the Levites. But the Apostle anticipates this objection by saying, that tithes were paid to the Levites only for a time, because they did not live: but that Melchizedek, because he is immortal, retains even to the end what has been given to him by God."

The editor, Rev. John Owen, adds this comment: "The obvious meaning of this verse is given by Calvin. The Levites were dying men, which shewed the character of their office; Melchizedek is represented as not dying, which betokens that his office as a priest, is perpetual." The tribute to the priesthood was only a temporary right of the Levites, it will be noted Calvin claims, and that it is the perpetual right of the priesthood which is after the order of Melchizedek. How clear and luminous is this interpretation when compared with that of many who stumble around over that verse and pretend not to be able to see just how it fits into the Apostle's argument. It seems to me that we strike the most triumphant of all the notes in this great address to the Hebrews in this very verse. Our High Priest has as His type one that liveth. This is preparing the way for the "power of an endless life" and "He ever liveth" which come later on in the chapter. We are dealing with that which has no end, which is true as much in respect to the tithes paid as to any other part of this divine arrangement. Any claim that the Levites had was only for the time. Any claim that Christ has had is living, is perpetual and no posterior grant can make it null and void. Here, then, we have a strong and inconvertible statement of the claim that Christ has on the tithe and that at just the point where we might be led to expect it. It seems to me that a man must be hunting for something when he passes this by and cries out for proof.

It may be worth while to call attention to this fact that the oldest Babylonian reference shows that the tithe was centuries before in force in the near vicinity of this same Melchizedek and that it is not any longer a question where Abraham got his idea of a tithe.

Rev. Henry Constable also makes this further point which is worth notice. The tithe is not ceremonial as is shown by the fact that "no part" of Jacob's offering "was for the use of the priesthood. The priest of Jacob's household was Jacob himself. When there was no ministry to support it was yet God's claim and accorded to Him."

It scarcely seems necessary to prolong this discussion. The universality of the tithe, as a moral obligation, seems to me to be beyond question. It is the universal minimum of the race in the matter of giving to the gods and the conclusion seems inevitable that it is the original requirement of God. Forms, materials, and incidents of giving may have varied, but the standard never. There does not appear any satisfactory reason for believing that it does not survive the changes from the Old to the New Dispensation. The voluntary tithe was recognized and urged on all hands until in the sixth century A. D. The general confusion of Church and State and everything else that followed gradually took away its voluntary character. It became a sort of enforced tribute to that monstrous duality which presided with such mock dignity over all interests, sacred and otherwise, until the time of reformation when divine truth and order began once more to appear. In all the mighty overturnings of the era of Wickliffe, Luther, Calvin and Knox, these "stalwart old iconoclasts" all contended for the tithe. While they lashed unmercifully the lazy monks and worldly clergy, yet with Wickliffe they preferred "the good old custom of paying tithes, according to one's own free-will, to good and godly men, who were able to preach the gospel."

Possibly it would be well to say of Selden who is generally quoted as opposed to the tithe, that he himself says of his famous book, "It was not written to prove that tithes are not due by the Law of God.... Neither is it anything else but itself, that is, a mere narration, and the Historie of Tithes." It comes out in the course of the narrative, however, that he was contending for the voluntary tithe, just as has been done in this discussion. He was suffering, as many others like him have suffered, from the oppression of human enactment and perversion in respect to that which God intended to be a gracious and wholesome provision. Hence arises the odium which attaches to the word tithe. But odium is not enough to excuse the retention of a principle represented by a name. Like the name Christian which we bear, it can by God's help be made an honorable one. It was so perverted in the time of the kings of Israel, as God had warned them it would be. Hezekiah, however, restored its proper usage. The tithe was never intended for a national tax to support the State. Its support was at first voluntary as it seems (1 Sam. 10:27). It came to be a fixed tribute by the demand of such kings as Rehoboam. It is to be remembered that odium, and perversion, and the plea of heavy taxes, did not prevent Malachi from accusing the whole Jewish nation of robbing God. The tithe is still holy to Him and ought to be brought into His house and must, if large blessings are to come.

The facts adduced lead inevitably to the main conclusions reached, if I understand the principles of logical induction. This method of induction is quite popular at present, when applied to certain historical data. I am persuaded that if as much surplus ingenuity and lauded scholarship were expended on these data as are expended on other data to establish useless hypotheses, the Church of God would be more edified and would become "liberal" in a manner more pleasing to God. Strictness in doctrine and liberality in giving surely are more compatible with divine teaching than liberality in doctrine and stinginess in giving. Liberality has affected the wrong thing. The slackening of doctrinal teaching has benefited nothing, but has brought a flood of Rationalism, Infidelity, and Unbelief on the Church. Loosen the purse strings and cherish "the faith once delivered to the saints" as God gave it, and we have His word that the floods of evil shall be driven back by the floods of heavenly blessings which He challenges us to receive.

The sweep of the facts is broad. The conclusions are inevitable. The tithe is universal. Its duty remains to be performed. It seems an unnecessary trespass on time and patience to try to meet all the quibbles that may be started. It is not time for sentiment, nor is it well to bring in the poor, as if God did not know how to provide for them. Pastors know that the poor are not the grumblers. Many complain against the law that the one-seventh of time is God's. The Sabbath is not counted a burden, neither is it annulled on that account. Complaint settles nothing. People complain of everything under the sun and often of things above the sun. We are not called upon to adjust the relations of capital and labor which make the Sabbath and the Tithe an oppression (if you please to call them such), in order to prove the obligation of the Sabbath and the Tithe. One-seventh of time and one-tenth of money belong to the Lord. Who takes either for his own robs God, His word being witness. The same question arises as to why both are not more distinctly taught in the New Testament. Both are old and well established. Each is a minimum demanded without reservation. If this be not true of the tithe, then there is no law governing that grace of God in which we are to abound, unless it be that we should hold with some of the Fathers that "those who have received liberty should set aside all their possessions for the Lord's purpose." This is the only other method that has the much demanded New Testament approval, so far as amount is concerned. I do not find even our brethren who are so strenuous for New Testament teaching and practice, falling over themselves to adopt this method. Our own denomination is reckoned as a liberal one, but counting its income according to government reports which place the average income of every man, woman, and child at 55 cents per day, we have never paid for all purposes more than one-third of one-tenth of our income into the Lord's treasury. Some other branches of the Church may be a little better, but many of them are unquestionably worse. Well might Chrysostom exclaim, "O what a shame! that what was no great matter among the Jews should be pretended to be such among Christians!" Instead of giving a tithe, we fall so far below it that the tithe actually seems visionary to us. The most careful calculations show very clearly that God knows how much money he wants for His work and that with the tithe of the Church's income at present, the world could be evangelized in this generation. The early Christians gave often all their means and all their time. We complain of one-seventh of time and one-tenth of money. If the Jews could give 25 per cent from the produce of Judean hills and valleys, why cannot we give cheerfully at least one-tenth to the kingdom of Him who though He was rich yet for our sakes became poor that we through His poverty might be rich? He who falls below one-fourth gives less than the Jew. Having a better covenant, established on better promises, and administered by a better Mediator, shall we grumble at one-tenth, the tribute of a heathen or savage to a god he dreads and with no spark of divine love to call forth his offering? To fail to pay the tithe is not only worse than Jewish but even worse than heathenish. Nowhere do we find such niggardliness, no not even in a heathen.

No one has ever been the worse off for doing his duty toward God. "The Path to Wealth" by "A Blacksmith" contains a chapter of voluntary testimonies given at a public meeting. Twenty-nine testimonies were given either directly or indirectly. The occupations of the persons were as follows: Five not named, six ministers, four farmers, two merchants, and one each of the following: General agent, Y. M. C. A. secretary, student, clerk, lady stenographer, principal of schools, shoemaker, young lady telegraph operator who had a mother and sister to support, and a missionary from India, who told the story of one of his native helpers, Bhelsari Naiah, who had been tithing for three months when this conversation took place. "Well, Bhelsari, how does the tithing system work?" "Capitally, sir." "Ah, how is that? You were always complaining of being hard up, and even in debt, when you used your whole income for self; now, you give one-tenth to God, you have no complaints." "Ah, sir, the nine-tenths, with God's blessing, is better far than the ten-tenths used to be without it." I have received many testimonies to the same effect. Mr. Thomas Kane, of Chicago, has had thousands and thousands of such replies, so that we may safely say that Bhelsari's answer must stand as the voice of general experience.

Not only have men tried it for themselves, but it has been tried in business where firms have kept a strict account of the Lord's part and disbursed it for charity and have not found the Lord's promise wanting. Of late years it has come to be a prominent part in the system of finance of various congregations. What is known as the Tithe Covenant Plan originated in Wesley Chapel in Cincinnati about eight years ago. The central idea of this plan is based upon the literal interpretation of Mal. 3:10, "Bring ye the whole tithe into the storehouse, etc." The members bring in every week in an unmarked envelope the tithe of their income for that week and all is counted together and then distributed by the officers of the Church according to a previously arranged schedule. This congregation, being a downtown one, was about to give up from lack of support, when this plan was started and now it is one of the most active churches in that city and is the most liberal of any church in the city or conference in its support of charity and missions.

The Third United Presbyterian Church of Chicago adopted this plan April 1, 1901. The Methodist Church of Shelbyville, Ind., adopted it on June 1, 1901. The Memorial Presbyterian Church of Indianapolis, Ind., adopted it on July 1, 1901. These were the churches that had made actual trial of it, when the Tithe Conference was held at Winona in August, 1902. Since then several have taken it up, notably the Delaware Avenue Baptist Church of Buffalo, N. Y., and the Eighth Presbyterian Church of Chicago. Mr. Blynn Yates of Buffalo, N. Y., has consented to act as the distributer of information in respect to the working of this plan and after the Conference at Winona this year literature will be issued which will give data concerning what some of us believe promises to be a mighty factor in the Church's progress in the years to come. In all these congregations where this plan has been given a fair trial it has wrought wonders and the testimonies that will soon be at your disposal will be a revelation, I judge, to many who have been in despair almost over the problem of financing the kingdom. It will show that God has a plan and that the plan will meet the needs of the Church to-day, as it always has in the past, when honestly administered. No congregation need fear to give it a fair trial. As the colored preacher said, "I hab nebber known a church killed by too much gibbin to de Lawd. If der should be such a church, and I should know about it, I'll tell you what I'd do. I'd go to dat church, and I'd clamber up its moss-covered roof, and I'd sit straddle of its ridge pole, and I'd cry aloud, 'Blessed am de dead dat die in de Lawd.'" If any one tries this method and faithfully proves the Lord therewith, and then goes under, it certainly will be time to say, "Blessed am de dead dat die in de Lawd."

Many give more than the tenth and should do so. I know some who give one-fifth, and higher proportions up to that height attained by one whom it has been my privilege to meet who gives nine-tenths of his income and lives on the one-tenth. When we have paid our due to the Lord, we still have nine-tenths out of which to meet the call of the gospel in such words as these, "Give good measure. Freely ye have received, freely give. Abound in this grace. Sell that thou hast and give to the poor." A man once gave such a large gift to missions as to call forth words of surprise. He said, "It is one-quarter of what I own. I found that as I was prospered my money engrossed more and more of my thoughts. I am not going to be a slave to the money God gave me, and I am going to conquer the love of money by giving it away." That was in accord with the word of Christ to the rich young ruler and any one who is becoming a slave of money ought not only to give a tenth, but might better give a quarter or a half or even all his money away, rather than die as the fool died who laid up treasure for himself and was not rich toward God. Christ commended the widow who gave all and cared for her as he will for all who honor Him with their substance. The tithe has been given by all races and conditions in the past and no objection on account of race or condition can hold against it now.

While we might have cut short much debate by saying that the tithe is not a Jewish institution but is an ancient law of the race and we are no more called upon to prove its obligation than we are that of the law of the Sabbath or of marriage, yet we have tried to present the case as briefly and yet thoroughly as possible within reasonable limits. But, as I said at Winona last year, suppose you deny all this evidence and refuse to be convinced of its obligation, there is one plea that you cannot gainsay. It is the one system that has never failed to get the money. The history of the past shows this. The enemies of the Evangelical Church recognize it. The Mormons, the Seventh Day Adventists, the Dowieites all find the tithe sufficient to carry on their wonderful propagandas and demonstrate the argument that God's tenth if rightly used by His Church would enable us soon to take the world for Christ. All other methods of raising money pale into insignificance when compared with this which has always, in all ages, and among all classes of peoples proved sufficient to do great things in the name of the religion or irreligion in behalf of which it was used. The simple argument, It works, ought to appeal to the many struggling Church workers who are at their wits' end to know how to meet expenses. That mere tithe-paying will bring spiritual blessing, I do not claim. The reverse is true, as the Pharisee testifies. But tithing according to God's plan and in the spirit which He has laid down in His word must and will bring great blessing.

One of our missionaries in India tells of a native who was an earnest Christian and a believer in tithing. He had a friend who was converted and he was anxious to have him tithe also. After some effort to persuade him and seemingly without avail, he gave his friend a sound thrashing and enforced the tithe by brawn and not by persuasion of conscience. This was zeal without knowledge. You can no more make a man give than you can make him pray. You can make a man say words, but it is not prayer. You may make him hand out money unwillingly, but that is not giving as I view it. I like to define giving as follows: Giving is a cheerful, willing, liberal, intelligent, quiet, regular and prayerful exercise of a God-given grace. This grace of giving, like all God's gifts, comes with the asking and stays with the using. It is no more possible for a man to have the grace of giving without asking for it and making proper use of it, than it is to have the Spirit for service without asking for and making use of that gift. I would not attempt to force this system on any unprayerful person or people. But, Oh that the Church might awake to its glorious provision and its wonderful privilege in this conformity to the law of giving! When a man asks for the grace of giving and receives the impulse to open his purse to abound in this grace, then comes to him God's rule, The Tenth is holy unto Me as a first-fruit of this grace, and immediately he begins to see where it is that a man crosses over the boundary line of selfishness and steps into the plane of devotion to God, and he takes the step and rejoices in it. As he walks on in the glad consciousness of duty done, he begins to rejoice in larger manifestations of this grace and meets other and larger opportunities for the gospel's sake and for the Master's sake, and thus the fulness of the blessing of this grace flows into his soul and he knows the meaning of abounding in this grace also.

What has been said of individual experience, may be just as truly said of the experience that comes to any congregation that will follow this same plan of

God, as some of our congregations can testify. The blessing is not only financial, but it is spiritual in a large and increasing sense. Would that John Knox might stir up the ministry now as he is said to have done in his day in Scotland when he said, "There is no impiety against which it is more requisite you set yourselves in this time. Repent, therefore, and amend your own neglect in this behalf and call upon others for amendment." Max Mueller is said also to have written to a young minister, "When one thinks what this world of ours would be, if at least this minimum of Christianity were a reality, one feels that you are right in preaching this simple duty in season and out of season, until people see that without fulfilling it, every other profession of religion is a mere sham."

The ringing words of Bishop Potter at the dedication of Grace Chapel in New York city, while they may apply peculiarly to the Episcopal Church, yet are wholesome words to all God's people.

"The growth of wealth and of luxury, wicked, wasteful, and wanton, as before God I declare that luxury to be, has been matched step by step by a deepening and deadening poverty which has left whole neighborhoods of people practically without hope and without aspiration. At such a time, for the church of God to sit still and be content with theories of its duty outlawed by time and long ago demonstrated to be grotesquely inadequate to the demands of a living situation, this is to deserve the scorn of men and the curse of God! Take my word for it, men and brethren, unless you and I and all those who have any gift or stewardship of talents, or means, of whatsoever sort, are willing to get up out of our sloth and ease and selfish dilettanteism of service, and get down among the people who are battling amid their poverty and ignorance—young girls for their chastity, young men for their better ideal of righteousness, old and young alike for one clear ray of the immortal courage and the immortal hope—then verily the church in its stately splendor, its apostolic orders, its venerable ritual, its decorous and dignified conventions, is revealed as simply a monstrous and insolent impertinence!"

Seeing that this indictment is well placed, why should not any person or people pay to God at least the tenth, as His minimum requirement? The need has not ceased. We have the poor with us. The ministry is appointed to live by the gospel. The field is not Judea alone, but the world. Opportunities of beneficence are multifold. Men are waiting and hungering for the gospel. Men are longing to take it to them. Means we must have. Our greatest need, as before stated, from the human side is money, not men or machinery.

As Mr. Gladstone said, "The inculcation and practice of systematic beneficence will prove the moral specific for this age." Will the people rob God? "Bring ye the whole tithe into the storehouse, that there may be meat in mine house, and prove me now herewith, saith the Lord of hosts, if I will not open you the windows of heaven and pour you out a blessing, that there shall not be room enough to receive it." Why not make the test? Then God even our own God will bless us with the riches of His grace, to whom be glory in the Church of Jesus Christ throughout all ages, world without end. Amen.

FOOTNOTES:

[A] Yes, I know the stock answer to this. "Jacob's Vow." But what and where was Jacob when he used this language? A sneak and a fugitive from the just wrath of his brother. It is safe to say that never afterwards, certainly never after he became an honest man did he speak of or regard the payment of the Tithe as a "gift" to God. It looks as though the Pharisee boasted of giving Tithes, but there is no use in painting him blacker than he was. Let us hope he had in mind that he gave tithes to the Temple service, in which case the word he used was correct. It is unfair to charge even him with claiming that he gave Tithes to God. So far as I recall Christ never mentioned Tithes but twice. Once He said "Ye tithe;" in the other instance "Ye pay tithes," and added his approval.

[B] After the above was written, the following came to my notice from Prof. Sayce in a late work entitled, "The Religions of Ancient Egypt and Babylonia." In speaking of the custom of the authorities, he says, "A tithe of all that the land produced was theirs, and it was rigorously exacted, for the support of the temples and priests. Babylonia, in short, was the inventor of the tithe."